At David C Cook, we equip the local church around the corner and around the globe to make disciples. Come see how we are working together—go to **www.davidccook.com**. Thank you!

KNOWING THE HOLY SPIRIT

DAVID C COOK FAMILY DEVOTIONS

KNOWING THE HOLY SPIRIT

52 Devotions to Grow Your Family's Faith

DAVID C COOK

transforming lives together

KNOWING THE HOLY SPIRIT
Published by David C Cook
4050 Lee Vance Drive
Colorado Springs, CO 80918 U.S.A.

Integrity Music Limited, a Division of David C Cook
Eastbourne, East Sussex BN23 6NT, England

The graphic circle C logo is a registered trademark of David C Cook.

LCCN 2018931611
ISBN 978-1-4347-1251-6
eISBN 978-0-8307-7576-7

© 2018 Beers Family Real Estate LLC
Published in association with the literary agency of
Mark Sweeney & Associates, Naples, FL 34113.

The Team: Lindsay Black, Jeff Gerke, Rachael Stevenson, Jane Ann Kenney
Cover Design: Nick Lee
Cover Illustration: Oliver Genoux

Printed in the United States of America
First Edition 2018

1 2 3 4 5 6 7 8 9 10

062818

CONTENTS

NOTE TO PARENTS

You are about to begin a delightful journey with a child, using this book as your road map. Whether you are a parent, grandparent, uncle, aunt, teacher, neighbor, or some other special person with the great privilege of leading children God's way, praise God for you.

This is a devotional book to help children—*and* you—know the Holy Spirit better, love Him more deeply, and serve Him more effectively.

The first section in every devotion is a poetry-style passage to read aloud to your child. This is designed to engage your child with the opening Bible verse in a way that lights their imagination and touches their hearts.

The "Grow Your Faith" section is for you to read to yourself, perhaps before you sit down with your child. This section leads you to interact with the passage and some aspect of the Holy Spirit in a way that may challenge and inspire you. This could help prepare you if the other parts of the reading give rise to a discussion with your child.

This is followed by a section called "Grow Your Child's Faith." This is also designed to be read aloud to your child. It extends the original thought and brings application in ways he or she can use in real life.

Each devotion concludes with a suggested prayer your child could say to the Holy Spirit. If a prayer isn't exactly what your child is thinking or feeling right then, encourage him or her to adjust it so it becomes an authentic expression to God.

It is our prayer that as you and your child learn more about the Holy Spirit, you will forge an unforgettable bond in which your hearts and God's heart become knitted together in love.

THE HOLY SPIRIT IS CREATOR

In the beginning God created the heavens and the earth. Now the earth was formless and empty, darkness was over the surface of the deep, and the Spirit of God was hovering over the waters.

Genesis 1:1–2

Something from nothing,
everything from nothing.
From microbes to galaxies,
from honeybees to you and me.

The Lord God made it all …
Father, Son, and Holy Spirit.
If God's Spirit can do that,
what can He do with you?

Grow Your Faith

Before you came alive in Christ, you were dead in sin. Like the earth before the Spirit moved, your life was chaotic and dark. In the Spirit, you come to life. The same work the Spirit did at creation, He does in you, recreating you to live a new life.

Grow Your Child's Faith

When you read the Bible verses above, what picture comes to your mind? God saw the possibility of life. He made that possibility into reality through His Spirit. He sees possibility in you too. Will you let the Holy Spirit work in your life?

Holy Spirit, what was it like to hover over the earth when it looked like that? Thank You for making it! Amen.

THE HOLY SPIRIT STIRS CREATIVITY

"I have filled Bezalel with the Spirit of God and have given him
the skill, ability, and knowledge to do all kinds of work. He is
able to design pieces to be made from gold, silver, and bronze."
Exodus 31:3–4 NCV

If you want to be great at anything,
from art to sports to friendship,
you start with what God's Spirit gave you,
and you add practice, learning, and time.

Everything you do really, really well
is actually a dance between you and God.
His Spirit gives to you and you give back,
and between you, beauty is born.

Grow Your Faith

What level of masterpiece could your child become if you partnered with God's Spirit in that loving, artistic dance? His Spirit has made you a creative genius to love your little one. What will you "paint" today?

Grow Your Child's Faith

If someone is really good at art or singing or sports, is it because they were born good at that thing or because they worked really hard to get better? Or both? God's Spirit gave you some amazing abilities, and He can't wait to see how high you can take those things with practice and training.

Holy Spirit, please help me find the things You've made me good at and get better at using them—and then please show me how to help others with them. Amen.

3

THE HOLY SPIRIT
GIVES POWER

The LORD took some of the Spirit Moses had,
and he gave it to the seventy leaders.
Numbers 11:25 NCV

When you give away all the cookies
in your basket,
you're out of cookies.

But when God's Spirit gives gifts,
there's enough to go around,
and each one has a purpose.

What gifts and abilities
has the Holy Spirit given you?

Grow Your Faith

The Spirit fills us and flows onto other people, not like one cup of water but like a gushing spring. The best way to experience more of the Spirit is to give away as much as you can. Who can you pour God's gifts out upon today?

Grow Your Child's Faith

With your parent, light one candle, and then use that candle to light one more—or two or ten! Did the first candle get weaker every time it lit another one, or is it burning just as bright as before? That's how the gifts of God's Spirit are: when you give them to others, you have just as much as you started with!

Holy Spirit, just like that candle spread light and heat to others, I want to spread You to everyone I meet. I know You will never run out! Amen.

THE HOLY SPIRIT INSPIRES SCRIPTURE

*"The Spirit of the LORD spoke through me;
his word was on my tongue."*
2 Samuel 23:2

There will be moments in your life
when you absolutely know
God is working through you.

Maybe you'll suddenly get an idea
that seemed to come from nowhere
and ends up being the perfect solution.

Maybe you'll feel a powerful need
to go find out how someone is doing,
and they'll say, "How did you know?"

Maybe you'll find yourself saying something
you hadn't planned to say,
but it is exactly what someone needs to hear.

Those are the moments—the inspiration—we live for.
This is how the Bible was written!

Grow Your Faith

The more you listen to God's Spirit and meditate on His Word, the more often you'll get to enjoy these moments.

Grow Your Child's Faith

Reading God's Word might give you some ideas about things the Holy Spirit would like you to do. What are you waiting for? Ask God right now what He'd like you to get up and do or say. And then do it!

Holy Spirit, I want to be one of the people You pick to help someone else. Please send me! Amen.

5

THE HOLY SPIRIT IS AN ARCHITECT

He gave him the plans of all that the Spirit had put in his mind for the courts of the temple of the LORD.
1 Chronicles 28:12

God's Spirit planned and created
the universe.
And then that same Spirit handed over
the plans to a temple.

How amazing do you think
that temple was?
How amazing do you think
God's plans for *you* are?

Grow Your Faith

Just like God had a specific plan for how He wanted the temple built, He has specific plans for you. And He has specific plans for how He'd like you to raise up your child as a temple of the Holy Spirit. How can you discern those plans?

Grow Your Child's Faith

Do you know what a blueprint is? What about a recipe? Maybe an instruction manual? Some things need to be made in exactly the right way for them to turn out how they're meant to. You are one of those things, and the Bible is your guidebook!

Holy Spirit, what plans do You have for me? I can't wait to find out! Amen.

THE HOLY SPIRIT CREATED YOU

*"The Spirit of God has made me; the breath
of the Almighty gives me life."*
Job 33:4

In the Bible, the word for *spirit*
also means "wind" and "breath."

So … the Spirit of God
made you,
and the Breath of God
gives you life.

Every breath,
from first to last,
is a daily gift.
What will you do with your breaths?

Grow Your Faith

If you or someone you know struggles with a breathing disorder, then you know how precious breath is. May we increase in our awareness that the presence—moving in and out, second by second—of the Holy Spirit is just as vital to life.

Grow Your Child's Faith

When God was ready to bring Adam to life, He breathed into him, and Adam opened his eyes. You have that same breath of God inside you. You are a miracle of God's own making. What do you think God wants you to do today?

Holy Spirit, it seems like You filled me with Yourself to do amazing things in the world. Please show me one way I can spill out Your love to someone today. Amen.

THE HOLY SPIRIT IS WITH YOU

"I will go with you and give you peace."
Exodus 33:14 CEV

God the Father is all around,
always loving and watching.
Jesus sits at His right hand,
telling God how much He loves us.

The Holy Spirit
is how both God and Jesus
stay *inside* us and *beside* us
every minute of every day.

Grow Your Faith

Sometimes we ask, "God, where were You when that tragedy happened and I was afraid?" We know right where He was. The Holy Spirit's presence goes and stands with believers at *all* times. He may not have intervened, but He never abandoned you.

Grow Your Child's Faith

It can be confusing to think about how the Holy Spirit is different from God and Jesus. We like to be able to understand everything, but we cannot understand God! How can God be three but also one? It's a mystery, and that's okay! We shouldn't be able to understand God because He is just so awesome. Over and over again, the Bible tells us that the Spirit empowers God's people. We don't have to understand perfectly in order to be thankful God is with us and helping us.

Holy Spirit, I don't totally understand how it all works, but I know that when I pray to You or God the Father or Jesus, all of You hear me and love me! Amen.

THE HOLY SPIRIT IS EVERYWHERE

Where can I go to get away from your Spirit?
Where can I run from you?
Psalm 139:7 NCV

How would you like
to play hide and seek
with God?
You'd lose every time.

We don't *want* to run from God.
But even if we did want to,
we couldn't.
God's Spirit is *everywhere*.

Grow Your Faith

Occasionally, like when we know we're sinning, we can wish God's Spirit *wasn't* everywhere. But it is for our good that He sees all—even the stuff we'd rather no one ever see. It means He's always right there when we're ready to restore our relationship with Him.

Grow Your Child's Faith

It wouldn't be any fun to play hide and seek with God. But it's good that we can never hide from Him. It means He always sees us, always listens to us, always knows how we feel, and always loves us. *Always.*

Holy Spirit, when I do something wrong, I kind of don't want You seeing me. But I'm glad I can always come back to You and You always know where I am. Amen.

THE HOLY SPIRIT GRIEVES

*Then the LORD's people turned against him
and made his Holy Spirit sad.*
Isaiah 63:10 CEV

God the Father is heartbroken
when people disobey Him.

Jesus wept
at the grave of Lazarus.

It shouldn't surprise us then
that the Holy Spirit can get sad too.

Grow Your Faith

How do we turn against God? It has to be sin that counts as rebellion against Him. It hurts when someone we love attacks us and shows resentment instead of affection. Is there some area of your life in which you're spurning God's love?

Grow Your Child's Faith

When your parents ask you to do chores or your homework and you argue and go slow and hope they'll forget about it, you make them sad. One way to be sure you're making the Holy Spirit happy is to obey your parents or teachers when they ask you do to something, even if it isn't your favorite thing to do.

Holy Spirit, I never want to make You sad. Please help me obey my parents as if I'm really obeying You! Amen.

THE HOLY SPIRIT CAUSED THE HOLY BIRTH

"Joseph son of David, do not be afraid to take Mary home as your wife, because what is conceived in her is from the Holy Spirit."
Matthew 1:20

Throughout history,
the only baby *ever*
made without a human father
was Jesus.

The Holy Spirit created life
in the garden of Eden,
and He created life
in Mary.

Grow Your Faith

If you had been Joseph and heard Mary tell you God had made her pregnant, would you have believed her? No one would have, most likely, without God intervening to reveal the truth. Is there something you don't believe about God right now that might actually be true?

Grow Your Child's Faith

Mary must have been afraid to become a mother. After all, no one had ever become a mom like she would. But the Holy Spirit's work didn't stop with giving her Jesus. He stayed with Mary all the time, to help her be the best mom she could be.

Holy Spirit, it's incredible to me that You gave a woman a baby that was both God and human. What other incredible things can You do? Would You do some of them in my life? Amen.

BAPTISM IS DONE IN THE NAME OF THE HOLY SPIRIT

*"Go and make followers of all people in the world. Baptize them
in the name of the Father and the Son and the Holy Spirit."*
Matthew 28:19 NCV

Have you been baptized?
The water represents Jesus' blood
washing you clean.
It's a way of showing that you love Jesus.

All three parts of God—
Father, Son, and Spirit—
are there, watching and clapping,
whenever anyone is baptized.

Grow Your Faith

Baptism is meant as a way for a believer to proclaim his or her faith in Jesus to the world. Have you been baptized? If not, what has gotten in the way of doing it? What steps will you take next to be baptized?

Grow Your Child's Faith

God asks every one of His children to show the whole world that they love Him, and baptism is how He asks us to do it. There's nothing magical about baptism. If you want to know more about baptism, ask an adult. They'll be happy to help!

Holy Spirit, You made the invisible God into a visible baby, and You ask me to make my invisible faith in You visible to the world by being baptized. That is awesome! Amen.

THE BIBLE IS INSPIRED BY THE HOLY SPIRIT

All Scripture is God-breathed.
2 Timothy 3:16

The Bible we have today
was written by people
being told what to write
by the Holy Spirit.

How incredible would it be
to know that something you're writing
was straight from God
and would last forever?

Grow Your Faith

Some people like to ignore whole sections of the Bible that don't match what they want to believe. It's hard to do this when you agree that it *all* came from God. We need to stay humble and realize maybe we just don't understand all of the Bible yet. We can ask God for wisdom, and He loves to give it (see James 1:5)!

Grow Your Child's Faith

If God appeared in your room and handed you a letter He wrote, would you read it? Guess what? That's what the Bible is! Find one and start seeing what it's about.

Holy Spirit, You wrote the Bible, and You made the baby Jesus inside Mary. It seems like You're the way God does all the most important things. Amen.

THE HOLY SPIRIT WILL GIVE US WORDS TO SPEAK

"Whenever you are arrested and brought to trial, do not worry beforehand about what to say. Just say whatever is given you at the time, for it is not you speaking, but the Holy Spirit."

Mark 13:11

The Holy Spirit
gave God's words
to the people who wrote the Bible.

If you're ever on the spot
because of your love for Jesus,
the Holy Spirit will give you
God's words too!

Grow Your Faith

It seems that God leans forward when anyone who loves Him is "on trial" for faith. Have you ever been in such a spot? Did you ask God for help? Did He give you the right words and actions?

Grow Your Child's Faith

When you talk with your friends about Jesus, ask the Holy Spirit to help you know what to say. And He will!

Holy Spirit, show me someone to talk to about You, and please give me the right words! Amen.

THE HOLY SPIRIT CAN FILL US BEFORE WE ARE BORN

"He will be filled with the Holy Spirit even before he is born."
Luke 1:15

One special time
for one special baby
the Holy Spirit entered a person
before he was even born.

Before that baby was born,
he was named John.
He was the cousin and helper of Jesus,
and God's Spirit called John
to a special mission.

Grow Your Faith

God has a special mission for all of us. Some people, like John, seem to be born knowing that mission. Others spend many years fighting God before yielding to His will. Still others know only in hindsight what God was doing in their lives.

Grow Your Child's Faith

Do you know someone who is going to have a baby? Did you know you can pray for that baby already? That baby is precious to God, just like you are.

Holy Spirit, please help unborn babies be protected and born healthy and grow up with parents and families who will love them with all their hearts. Amen.

15

THE HOLY SPIRIT FILLS US

*Then his father, Zechariah, was filled with the
Holy Spirit and gave this prophecy.*
Luke 1:67 NLT

The Spirit of God
doesn't trickle into us.
He doesn't sprinkle a few drops.
He doesn't give us half a tank.

The Spirit of God
fills us
all the way up
to the very tip top.

Grow Your Faith

Paul said the only people who don't have the Holy Spirit are those
who are not Christians (see Rom. 8:9). The Holy Spirit fills us
at the moment of salvation. Does it change anything for you to
know that you are filled with God's own Spirit?

Grow Your Child's Faith

What does it mean that, if you are a Christian, you are *filled* with the Spirit of God? What will happen to a person who is a "container" of God? Especially if the container is so full the lid can't be put on it?

Holy Spirit, You fill me like a pot bubbling over on the stove. What amazing things do You want to do in me? Amen.

16

THE HOLY SPIRIT CAN REVEAL SECRETS

It had been revealed to him by the Holy Spirit that he
would not die before he had seen the Lord's Messiah.
Luke 2:26

Since God knows all secrets,
God's Spirit knows them all too.
Maybe once or twice, since He's inside us,
He'll tell some of what He knows.

Grow Your Faith

God sits outside our timeline the way we sit outside a closed novel.
If we've already read it, then we know what's going to happen
to the characters and we can think about them both before and
after they know the outcomes of their story. God knows all of that
about you too, and He smiled when He called you to Himself.

Grow Your Child's Faith

Would you want to know your future? It might be fun to know if you're going to get what you want for your birthday or what you'll do when you grow up. What if something really hard or painful was coming? Would you still want to know? Sometimes it's hard to remember that we aren't supposed to have all the answers yet.

Holy Spirit, sometimes I think it would be great to know the future. Thank You for knowing what's best! Amen.

17

THE HOLY SPIRIT IS LIKE A DOVE

The Holy Spirit descended on him in bodily form like a dove.
Luke 3:22

When God's Spirit first appeared
in a visible form,
He chose the shape of a dove.

A dove came back to Noah
with an olive branch
to show that land was near.

A dove was also a bird
used as a sacrifice for sins
by poor people in Bible times.

Grow Your Faith

God could have chosen any bird to descend on Jesus. Each choice would have suggested something about the Spirit. Why do you think the Spirit of God showed Himself as a dove?

Grow Your Child's Faith

If you could choose to be any kind of bird, what would it be? What do you like about that bird? Now think about the Holy Spirit. He could have appeared as any bird in the entire world, but He chose to appear as a dove. Why would the Spirit appear as a dove instead of a hawk or hummingbird or heron?

Holy Spirit, please teach me to be gentle and peaceful like a dove—like You. Amen.

18

THE HOLY SPIRIT LEADS US

*Jesus, full of the Holy Spirit, left the Jordan and
was led by the Spirit into the wilderness.*

Luke 4:1

We like to think of God leading us
to rivers and green fields.
But sometimes He leads us
into the desert.

Some lessons can be learned
only in the desert.
To be strong in the Lord,
we have to go there too.

Grow Your Faith

Wouldn't it be nice if we could learn everything we needed to
while staying in great health, having amazing relationships, and
earning enough money to stop worrying about it? Sadly, when
things are easy, we often forget to search for God. There's nowhere
like a desert—like massive debt, dying relationships, or chronic
illness—to make us cry out to God. No matter how near or far
God's blessings seem, the Holy Spirit is with you.

Grow Your Child's Faith

Deserts are hard places to live. It gets very hot during the day and very cold at night. Water isn't easy to find, and neither is food. Sometimes life will be very hard, and you might feel like you can't get what you need. Even worse, God might seem very far away. God is never far from you. The Holy Spirit watches over you and even lives in you when you believe in Jesus.

Holy Spirit, please help me when I am having a hard time. Remind me then that You are always near me and will always love me. Amen.

19

THE HOLY SPIRIT BRINGS JOY

Jesus, full of the joy through the Holy Spirit,
said, "I praise you, Father."
Luke 10:21

It's one thing to be happy
and something else to have joy.
Happiness is like a little ripple.
Joy from God is like a tidal wave.

When regular happiness fills you,
you might dance or shout or laugh.
But when the joy of God floods you,
who knows what awesome thing you'll do!

Grow Your Faith

The joy of the Lord comes from being filled with the Holy Spirit.
Is your life spilling over with the joy that can only come from
Him?

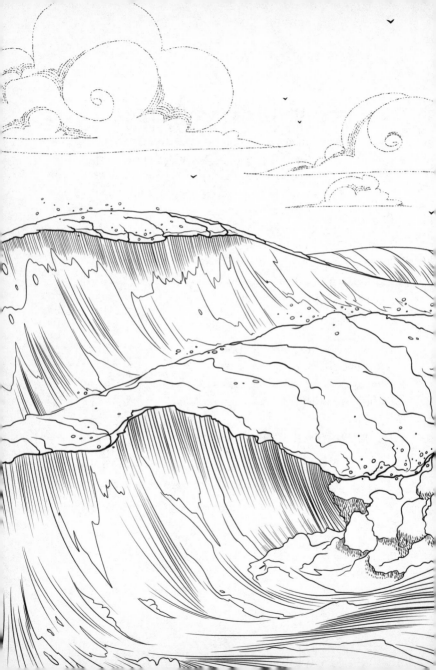

Grow Your Child's Faith

Sometimes we think we can only be joyful if we get everything we want. It really depends on what you want! If you want lots of toys and junk food and to watch as much TV as you can stand, it will never really give you joy. If you want to be full of the Holy Spirit, you can be joyful no matter what!

Holy Spirit, would You please fill me with Your joy? Fill me with Your power so I can help other people. Fill me with Your light, Your life, and Your words. Amen.

20

GOD THE FATHER WANTS TO GIVE US THE HOLY SPIRIT

"If you then, though you are evil, know how to give good gifts to your children, how much more will your Father in heaven give the Holy Spirit to those who ask him!"
Luke 11:13

Our parents can give really,
really good gifts.

For a birthday
or a holiday
or just because,
parents give good gifts.

If our parents, who aren't perfect,
can give us good things,
how much better are God's gifts for us?

Grow Your Faith

We receive the Holy Spirit when we come to faith. One purpose of Jesus' teaching here was to show that God longs to give good gifts to His children—gifts that are much more important and powerful than material things.

Grow Your Child's Faith

God is a Father who loves to give gifts to His children! He's not greedy or stingy. Why not ask Him for something? How can you be like Him and give to someone else?

Holy Spirit, You are the gift God put inside me! Thank You that You are generous and love to give. Amen.

21

THE HOLY SPIRIT TEACHES US

"The Holy Spirit will teach you at that time what you should say."
Luke 12:12

The Holy Spirit does many kinds of work.
He comforts and leads;
He warns and supplies our needs.

He also teaches
what God says
and what we can say
when we're not sure what to say.

Grow Your Faith

Who around you needs a word from God right now and you don't
have a clue what to say? Ask the Holy Spirit for wisdom.

Grow Your Child's Faith

Do you ever practice conversations in your head to get the words just right? Doing that can help you get over feeling nervous. The Holy Spirit also promises that He can give you the right words. If you are ever nervous about sharing the good news of Jesus with someone else, pray for the Holy Spirit's help. He's always ready to share the good news!

Holy Spirit, thank You for helping me know what I should say. Please give me the words I need when I need them. Amen.

22

THE HOLY SPIRIT REJECTS BLASPHEMY

"Anyone who speaks against the Son of Man can be forgiven, but anyone who speaks against the Holy Spirit will not be forgiven."
Luke 12:10 NCV

Jesus came as a man
and gave His life
to offer us forgiveness.
So what Jesus said in this verse
can be hard to understand.

Some people who hated Jesus
had just said that He,
the Son of God,
was actually a servant of the Devil.

Jesus' answer was that they could
say anything they wanted
against Him as a human
and God would forgive them.

But if they said that
the Holy Spirit
was really a demon,
God would not forgive that.

Grow Your Faith

It's tempting to believe that all people are good on some level. This verse suggests that some people really are not. They would prefer to speak evil against the Holy Spirit than to be led by Him!

Grow Your Child's Faith

It's hard to know what Jesus is saying here. But don't worry—you cannot accidentally speak against the Holy Spirit! Instead of worrying about this sin, pray the Holy Spirit will lead you and help you learn to give up *all* sins.

Holy Spirit, thank You for Your good work in the world. Help me spread the news about Your love everywhere I go. Amen.

23

THE HOLY SPIRIT GIVES SPIRITUAL LIFE

*"Humans can reproduce only human life, but the
Holy Spirit gives birth to spiritual life."*
John 3:6 NLT

People are very good
at learning.
God made us so curious!

We can learn so much
by studying in school
and reading a lot.

But only the Holy Spirit
can teach us spiritual truth
and grow spiritual life in us.

Grow Your Faith

Why are we here? This question can be answered with biological, sociological, historical, and other answers. However, the Spirit gives us spiritual answers. What has the Holy Spirit revealed to you about the "why" of life in Christ?

Grow Your Child's Faith

Jesus said the Holy Spirit is like the wind (John 3:8). When we ask Jesus into our hearts, the Spirit of God "blows" into our lives and fills us up. That's how we go from living a regular human life only and start living a godly life too.

Holy Spirit, I want You to always be the wind blowing in my life! Thank You for giving me new life! Amen.

24

THE HOLY SPIRIT REMINDS US OF JESUS' TEACHINGS

*"The Holy Spirit, whom the Father will send in my name, will teach
you all things and will remind you of everything I have said to you."*
John 14:26

Do you know someone
who can think of a song
for anything that happens
or give the perfect movie quote?

The Bible has a perfect quote
for every moment you could ever have
in your life.
And the Holy Spirit loves to speak them.

Grow Your Faith

God can use anything to speak to you. If you're listening to rock music, some of the lyrics may stand out to you because they're exactly what He wants to remind you of. But the Holy Spirit's favorite "source" to use is the Word of God itself. Consider memorizing ten new verses of Scripture and then see if He brings one or more to your mind at the perfect time.

Grow Your Child's Faith

Have you ever had a song stuck in your head? The next time that happens, listen to the part you keep singing, and see if maybe it's God trying to tell you something important.

Holy Spirit, I really want to hear You speak to me! Please catch my attention the next time You're doing it. Amen.

25

THE HOLY SPIRIT GUIDES US INTO TRUTH

*"But when he, the Spirit of truth, comes, he
will guide you into all the truth."*
John 16:13

When you're up high,
you can easily see
where things are below.

The view from the hill,
the bird's-eye view,
the satellite view …

They help you know
what to do
and where to go.

God's Spirit is like
a shepherd with
the ultimate view from above.

Grow Your Faith

What is truth? Pilate looked right at Jesus, truth incarnate, and asked that question. If he couldn't see truth when it was staring him in the face, what hope do we have in this world of political spin, agenda-driven journalism, and moral relativism? It's not a problem to God! More than ever, we have to rely on our Holy Spirit to shepherd us.

Grow Your Child's Faith

Think of a time when you were confused about something. Maybe you're confused about something now. Ask God's Spirit to guide you to what is true and right.

Holy Spirit, You are the Spirit of truth! Help me know Your voice and follow Your guiding. How amazing to have You, the perfect GPS, in my heart! Amen.

26

THE HOLY SPIRIT IS THE BREATH OF GOD

And with that he breathed on them and
said, "Receive the Holy Spirit."
John 20:22

Jesus breathed out,
and the Holy Spirit
came *in*.

What Jesus had carried
in Himself only,
is now given to us.

What had happened only in Jesus
now happens
in those who love Him.

Grow Your Faith

Read John 16:7 and explore any connections between that verse
and the one at the beginning of today's devotional.

Grow Your Child's Faith

Jesus is the only one to have ever walked the earth with God's Spirit inside Him fully and at all times. But when Jesus died and rose again, the time had come for every person who followed Him to be filled with God's Spirit fully and at all times. We have the same power and Spirit in us that Jesus had!

Holy Spirit, it's crazy to think that something only Jesus could do—have You inside Him while living a human life—is something I can do as a Christian! Please show me what that means. Amen.

27

THE HOLY SPIRIT BRINGS SPIRITUAL POWER

"You will receive power when the Holy Spirit comes on you."
Acts 1:8

It used to be that
when God wanted to do
something special with a person
the Holy Spirit would come on that person
and the results would be amazing.

Everything changed
with Jesus.

Now the Holy Spirit
always lives in God's people
to give us all the power we need,
all the time.

Grow Your Faith

The disciples were special and privileged, having been with Jesus, but they were still just ordinary people. They were similar to David, Noah, or Micah—Old Testament believers. But when the Holy Spirit came into the disciples, suddenly they were filled with the same power that had energized Jesus and brought Him back from the dead. And new horizons opened to them. What might be possible to you because you have God's Spirit that would be impossible to you without Him?

Grow Your Child's Faith

The next time you hear yourself saying, "I can't do that; I'm just a kid!" remember David fighting Goliath. And remember that you're "just" a kid who has the same power inside you that raised Jesus from the dead.

Holy Spirit, You are power! And You're inside me! That's a little scary but mostly exciting. What powerful things do You want to do in and through me? Let's do it! Amen.

28

THE HOLY SPIRIT CALLS

But before he was taken up, he gave orders to the apostles
he had chosen with the help of the Holy Spirit.

Acts 1:2 CEV

Sometimes when the Holy Spirit speaks
He says words of comfort.
He reminds and guides us.
He encourages and corrects us.

But sometimes He calls us
for a special mission.
How cool would it be
to be sent out on a God-mission?

Grow Your Faith

We can come to think of the Holy Spirit's ministry being limited to conviction of sin or reminders of God's Word, or perhaps to miracles and healing. But occasionally, God's Spirit lifts the curtain and lets us glimpse—or even join—what He's doing on the larger stage. Have you ever sensed God calling you in this way?

Grow Your Child's Faith

If God wanted to, He could just speak a word and anything He wanted to be done would be done—like He did when He created the world. But it seems like so much of what He does now is done through people He loves. Don't be surprised if the Holy Spirit calls you to do something that God wants done. It will be incredible!

Holy Spirit, I think it would be so amazing if You picked me for a special mission the same way You picked Barnabas and Saul. I'm right here, volunteering. Please send me! Amen.

29

THE HOLY SPIRIT
IS A GIFT

*"Repent and be baptized, every one of you, in the
name of Jesus Christ for the forgiveness of your sins.
And you will receive the gift of the Holy Spirit."*

Acts 2:38

You can't buy the Holy Spirit
at the store.
You can't earn the Holy Spirit
by being good.
You can't borrow the Holy Spirit
from anyone else.

But you can receive the Holy Spirit
as a gift.

Grow Your Faith

While the Holy Spirit—like salvation, for that matter—is a free gift, He doesn't come to us uninvited. He doesn't impose. Nor does He come until we declare Jesus is our Lord and believe in our hearts that God raised Jesus from the dead (see Rom. 10:9). Have you done what you needed to invite the Holy Spirit into your life?

Grow Your Child's Faith

God's Spirit is free, but He's not cheap. Jesus paid the most expensive price, so the Holy Spirit could be free for you and me. Because of what Jesus did on the cross, we can have the Holy Spirit living inside of us. We pay a price too—giving Jesus our lives. When we love Him, the Holy Spirit lives in us.

Holy Spirit, thank You that You come to me for free. I want You to live in me forever! Amen.

30

WE CAN (TRY TO) LIE TO THE HOLY SPIRIT

Then Peter said, "Ananias, how is it that Satan has so filled your heart that you have lied to the Holy Spirit and have kept for yourself some of the money you received for the land?"
Acts 5:3

It's hard to lie to the One
who knows everything,
including what's true
in your own mind.

But *telling* a lie isn't the same
as getting away with a lie.
We can tell a lie even if
the other person knows the truth.

Grow Your Faith

Sometimes we're tempted to make ourselves seem better than we are. Can you think of a time you lied to God? Most times, we end up lying to ourselves sooner than trying to lie to God. But maybe you made a promise to Him that you didn't—or never intended to—keep. Could you correct that now?

Grow Your Child's Faith

Have you ever seen a little kid tell a lie even when everyone knows what's actually true? That lie is silly, isn't it? The kid won't get away with it *and* he or she has done something wrong by telling the lie. In the same way, we're being pretty silly if we try to get away with anything less than the truth when it comes to God. Can you think of a lie you tried to tell Him?

Holy Spirit, I never want to lie to You or make promises to You that I can't or won't keep. Please help me be honest with You, even when I'm not doing the right thing. Thank You for loving me. Amen.

31

THE HOLY SPIRIT CAN'T BE BOUGHT

When Simon saw that the Spirit was given when the apostles laid
their hands on people, he offered them money to buy this power.
Acts 8:18 NLT

When the church was very young,
the Holy Spirit was sometimes given to a person
when an apostle put his hands on that person
and prayed.

There was a magician named Simon
who saw this happen
and wanted this power,
so he tried to buy it like a magic spell.

But it doesn't work that way.
The Holy Spirit's power is free.

Grow Your Faith

Simon recognized real power when he saw it. The miracles and signs that came when the apostles laid their hands on someone was far beyond any "magic" he'd ever encountered. Do you know of people who come to God for signs and magical miracles but don't embrace Him in their hearts?

Grow Your Child's Faith

People say that the best things in life can't be bought. They're free, but they're not worthless. A trip to the park with your friends might be one. Singing praises to God is another. Name some things that make your life great but can't be bought with money.

Holy Spirit, thank You for making Your best gifts free! Amen.

32

THE HOLY SPIRIT ENCOURAGES US

The church became stronger, as the Holy Spirit
encouraged it and helped it grow.
Acts 9:31 CEV

Did you know that the Holy Spirit
has lots of names?

One of these is Encourager.
What a great name for
the Spirit who encourages us!

Though He has many jobs,
The Holy Spirit loves His job as encourager.

Grow Your Faith

Where do you need encouragement right now? Ask the Holy
Spirit for some—He gives the best gifts!

Grow Your Child's Faith

Sooner or later, everyone, even the happiest person, gets sad. It can seem like nothing good is going to happen … ever. Disappointments and hurts come, and people can be mean. In all those times, the Holy Spirit wants to help you up, give you a strong hug, say the perfect thing to you, and send you out again with hope in your heart.

Holy Spirit, sometimes I'm really sad. It's amazing that You're there, always ready to cheer me up and love me back to my feet. Amen.

33

THE HOLY SPIRIT COMMANDS

While they were worshiping the Lord and going without eating, the Holy Spirit told them, "Appoint Barnabas and Saul to do the work for which I have chosen them."
Acts 13:2 CEV

God calls His children "soldiers of Jesus."
One thing every soldier has
is a commanding officer—a boss.

When the Holy Spirit called Barnabas and Saul,
He didn't ask the church to *think* about
setting those two men aside for this mission.

He told them to do it.
He commanded, and they obeyed.
The Spirit commands us too.

Grow Your Faith

The commands of God are like the commands a parent sets for a child. "Don't play in the street" is a command to keep children safe, as is "You shall not murder" (Ex. 20:13). Have you ever sensed the Holy Spirit commanding you to do something or *not* do something? He expects us to obey because obedience leads to what is best for us.

Grow Your Child's Faith

Parents, teachers, and others give us commands or rules for our good. When God gives a command, it's always going to work out for the best if we obey it. God's commands lead to His plans being done on earth.

Holy Spirit, sometimes I hear a rule or command I don't really want to obey. But I do love You and want to do the things that make You glad. Please help me obey. Amen.

I AM THE LORD YOUR GOD, YOU SHALL HAVE NO OTHER GODS BEFORE ME

THOU SHALT NOT MAKE UNTO THEE GRAVEN IMAGES.

YOU SHALL NOT USE THE LORD YOUR GOD'S NAME IN VAIN.

REMEMBER THE SABBATH DAY AND KEEP IT HOLY.

HONOUR YOUR FATHER AND MOTHER.

YOU SHALL NOT MURDER.

YOU SHALL NOT COMMIT ADULTERY.

YOU SHALL NOT STEAL.

YOU SHALL NOT BEAR FALSE WITNESS AGAINST YOUR NEIGHBOUR.

YOU SHALL NOT COVET ANYTHING THAT BELONGS TO YOUR NEIGHBOUR.

34

THE HOLY SPIRIT SENDS US TO DO HIS WORK

Barnabas and Saul were sent out by the Holy Spirit.
Acts 13:4 NLT

Have you ever just had the feeling
that you needed to do something?
Maybe you felt an urge
to go talk to someone or send a gift.

When we start listening to the Holy Spirit
and responding when He inspires us,
more and more we'll hear people ask,
"How did you know just what I needed?"

How *did* you know?
You heard it from the One
who knows every heart
and what each heart needs.

Grow Your Faith

Have you ever been on the receiving end of this sort of gift? For example, money arrives on the day you have a sudden financial need or someone uses the exact phrase you'd been wondering if God ever thought about you. Have you ever been on the giving or communicating side of such a message? How do these experiences make you feel?

Grow Your Child's Faith

If you think God is telling you to do something, and if that thing fits with what you know about Him and the Bible, take a chance and obey. And then see what happens!

Holy Spirit, please whisper things for me to do. I really want to be part of something You're doing to help other people. Amen.

35

THE HOLY SPIRIT CAN FILL US WITH JOY

The disciples were filled with joy and with the Holy Spirit.
Acts 13:52

There's peace,
and then there's the peace Jesus gives.
There's love,
and then there's love that passes understanding.

There's joy,
and then there's the
kind of joy
the Holy Spirit gives.

Grow Your Faith

This world has counterfeited every blessing God intends for His children. All of us yearn for love, joy, and peace. All of us yearn for meaning and purpose. Many try to achieve these things through worldly pursuits. But when we finally experience these as only God gives them, no substitute can ever satisfy again. Have you been filled with a blessing from the Holy Spirit?

Grow Your Child's Faith

If you had a toy that looked cool when you got it but fell apart right away, would you want more toys just like that, or would you choose toys less likely to break and leave you disappointed? That's how it is when we get the kind of joy God gives—after we get the best, the pretend kind we had been getting no longer seems that great.

Holy Spirit, please show me joy the way You mean joy to really be. Please show me love and peace and life the way You meant them to be. Amen.

36

THE HOLY SPIRIT RESTRAINS US

The Holy Spirit would not let them preach in Asia.
Acts 16:6 CEV

Sometimes the Spirit of God
asks us to do something.

And sometimes,
He asks us *not* to do something.

Grow Your Faith

Have you ever felt like God is telling you not to do or say something you'd been planning to do or say? Sometimes it's hard to tell if it's God's voice or your own. How can you tell when it's God's voice and when it's not?

Grow Your Child's Faith

What if you climb high in a tree so you can see the best path for your friends to take to stay safe? You call down directions, but your friends don't want to go the way you say. They can't see the danger you spotted or the amazing things they'll miss if they don't follow your plan. When God's Spirit tells us not to do something, it's because He knows what's best for us!

Holy Spirit, please help me know Your voice so well that I can tell right away when You are whispering for me to stop or go. I know You can see the road ahead and I can't. Amen.

37

THE HOLY SPIRIT WARNS US

"The Holy Spirit warns me that prison and hardships are facing me."
Acts 20:23

Since God knows the future,
He can give us a nudge
or a peek or a warning
about what might happen to us.

One thing we already know for sure
about the future?
God will be with us
all the time!

Grow Your Faith

Sometimes God warns His children through the Bible. Sometimes God warns His people through dreams. And sometimes God warns His people through His Spirit. When has the Spirit warned you? What form did that warning take? How did you respond?

Grow Your Child's Faith

Would you like to know what's going to happen to you in a week? Or in a year? Or in thirty years? Many stories have been written about what it might be like to know everything that's going to happen to us, but God gives us what we need to know exactly at the right time.

Holy Spirit, I don't know the future, but I know the One who does! Thank You that You'll be with me today and in the future, no matter what happens! Amen.

38

THE HOLY SPIRIT SPEAKS TRUTH

"The Holy Spirit spoke the truth to your ancestors."
Acts 28:25

One of the things we know
for sure about God
is that He is true.
Always.

People may lie to us
or stretch the truth
or make a promise
and not follow through.

But God will never, ever lie to you.
The Holy Spirit inside you
will only ever tell you
the truth.

Grow Your Faith

The people of Israel sometimes misunderstood what God was telling them. They thought the temple kept them safe, forgetting that the temple was only a symbol of the God who *actually* kept them safe. They also thought the Messiah would make Israel a new nation and throw off their oppressors. Instead, the Messiah did something much greater: He invited all people to enter the kingdom of heaven. If you're struggling with feeling God hasn't kept His promises, examine what promises He *actually* has made and what promises you *wish* He had made.

Grow Your Child's Faith

God has been telling the truth to people He loves for a long, long time. In fact, God has never, *ever* told a lie! Sometimes He says things you may not like, but you can trust what He says is true and part of His plan. Can you be the kind of friend who tells the truth?

Holy Spirit, I always want You to tell me what is true, even if I don't like it. Help me to tell my friends the truth too, with love and care. Amen.

39

GOD POURS OUT HIS LOVE THROUGH THE HOLY SPIRIT

God's love has been poured out into our
hearts through the Holy Spirit.
Romans 5:5

When God gave us the Holy Spirit,
He filled up our hearts
with love.

The Holy Spirit's love
is not a little bit.
It's not even just enough.

His love is amazing,
generous,
and enormous.

When the Holy Spirit
floods into our hearts,
so does God's love.

Grow Your Faith

The love of God wells up inside us through the Spirit. We may need God's love to fill us again and again so we can spill it out onto others, but we'll never "run out of love." As long as the Holy Spirit is in us, so is love.

Grow Your Child's Faith

How much does God love you? So much that the Holy Spirit comes to live inside you to remind you all the time that He loves you! He doesn't tell you once and expect you to remember. The Holy Spirit is always telling you about God's love. Can you hear Him?

Holy Spirit, I'm so glad I don't have to find love or build love or buy love to give to others. I could never do it, not for long and not enough. But You are love and You have filled me up so all I have to do is take some of You and let it flow out to people who need love! Amen.

40

THE HOLY SPIRIT GIVES US LIFE

*God raised Jesus from the dead, and if God's Spirit is living
in you, he will also give life to your bodies that die.*
Romans 8:11 NCV

We know God loves us.
We know that every day of our lives
He will be there for us.

But did you know
God will be there for us
when our lives end?

Jesus, who defeated death,
is in the life-giving,
death-defeating business.

The Holy Spirit in us
confirms that we will live
with Jesus.

Grow Your Faith

What a gift eternal life is! How can we thank God for it? The best way is to follow the leading of the Holy Spirit today, right now, to live lives worthy of God's people. On our own power, we cannot do this. But the Holy Spirit is always teaching us what true life is. Eternal life will be wonderful, and the promise that it is ours is so reassuring. Let that hope guide your life today.

Grow Your Child's Faith

Everyone who has Jesus inside them has the death-defeater inside them, because that's who Jesus is. Every Christian will live forever with God in heaven. We will get special new bodies—bodies that will never die.

Holy Spirit, it's so incredible to know I get to live forever in heaven with You! Amen.

41

THE HOLY SPIRIT BRINGS RIGHTEOUSNESS, PEACE, AND JOY

The kingdom of God is not a matter of eating and drinking,
but of righteousness, peace and joy in the Holy Spirit.
Romans 14:17

Have you ever been around someone
who was so strict about every rule
that you couldn't wait
to get away?

God is *not* like that.

The Holy Spirit gives us
goodness and peace and joy
that spill out
onto people around us.

Grow Your Faith

Do you tend to look down on people who have strict convictions? Or do you tend to condemn people who are more lenient? It's easy to fall into a pattern of judging people who aren't like us instead of accepting them and even learning from them. Are you letting temporary things distract you from the eternal?

Grow Your Child's Faith

If everyone was filled with the Holy Spirit, we wouldn't need laws. If God's love flowed out of every person, would anyone hurt anyone else on purpose? Or steal? Or cheat? Or lie? What's one rule in your house or school, or one law you know, that we wouldn't need if everyone was filled with love, peace, and joy?

Holy Spirit, please fill me with so much of Your goodness and joy that I treat everyone like You want me to. Amen.

42

GOD GIVES US THE HOLY SPIRIT TO SHOW HE ACCEPTS US

God, who knows the heart, showed that he accepted
them by giving the Holy Spirit to them.
Acts 15:8

After Jesus defeated death,
God's love went out
to all people.

He showed His love
to all of us
in the same way ...

by giving us His Holy Spirit!

Grow Your Faith

What are your normal, comfortable limits of who you call your Christian brothers and sisters? Consider whether those who make you uncomfortable, or who do Christianity "wrong," might also be among those God has approved.

Grow Your Child's Faith

There are kids like you, who love God just like you do, all over the world! Some of them don't even speak your language, but you'll get to be with them in heaven forever. Isn't that incredible?

Holy Spirit, it's amazing that I'll get to live forever with people I'll never meet on earth but who love You just as much as I do! Amen.

43

THE HOLY SPIRIT BRINGS HOPE

*May the God of hope fill you with all joy and
peace as you trust in him, so that you may overflow
with hope by the power of the Holy Spirit.*
Romans 15:13

Have you ever felt like everything
was going to end badly,
but then something changed
that gave you hope?

What if your family's car broke down
on a desert highway
where no cars came by for hours?
And then ... in the distance ... you saw a car coming!

Grow Your Faith

When we feel hopeless, our energy is gone. Why try? Why expend any effort? What's the point? It's all doomed to fail anyway. It's that feeling of being trapped that Jesus came to banish. Now, in Him, the oppressed are set free. Read and reflect upon Luke 4:18–19.

Grow Your Child's Faith

When we celebrate Jesus' birth, we celebrate that light came into the darkest of dark worlds, a world in which people had lost all hope. The candle, the birth of Jesus, grew brighter and brighter. The Holy Spirit spreads that light far and near through Jesus' followers. Now all the world can have hope. How can you bring this hope to someone you know?

Holy Spirit, You fill me with hope for this life and the next life. Please overflow me so people around me can see light in their darkness too. Amen!

44

YOU ARE THE TEMPLE OF THE HOLY SPIRIT

*Do you not know that your bodies are temples of
the Holy Spirit, who is in you, whom you have
received from God? You are not your own.*
1 Corinthians 6:19

God lives everywhere;
wherever He wants is His house.

The tabernacle, the temple, the church:
these are places God's people go to meet God,
but these places
do not hold God.

Did you know every Christian
is also a house of God?
If Jesus is in your heart,
then you're a temple too!

Grow Your Faith

When we walk into a temple or cathedral, the atmostphere tends
to be hushed and gives us a sense of awe. When the Holy Spirit
dwells within us, we are a sacred place—a noble house of the Lord.
Consider that with a hush and sense of awe.

Grow Your Child's Faith

When you walk into a beautiful museum or restaurant, or even someone's fancy house, do you go around trashing the place? Do you smash things and paint the furniture and rip it up? Of course not! Because your own body is the beautiful temple of God, you need to be sure you're treating *it* well too. Do you hurt your body? Do you feed it only junk food? Don't you clean and care for it? Treat the house of the Holy Spirit well!

Holy Spirit, help me see myself as an amazing house where You live, so I'll treat my body well. Please also help me see everyone around me as beautiful homes where You live or may one day live. Amen.

45

THE HOLY SPIRIT GIVES GIFTS

There are different kinds of spiritual gifts, but
they all come from the same Spirit.
1 Corinthians 12:4 CEV

Everybody is naturally good at something.
Usually more than one thing.
Maybe it's singing or sports
or building things or doing math.

God gives His children all kinds of gifts,
kind of like handing out tools
that He'll ask us to use
to build God's kingdom.

Those gifts are things like teaching,
planning, helping, hospitality,
encouraging, leading, giving,
or even believing God 100 percent.

Grow Your Faith

If you don't yet know your own spiritual gifts, consider taking a free spiritual gifts survey online. They have them for kids too. They may change over the years, but it's great to get an idea how God has crafted you, especially as you look for ways to serve in the local church.

Grow Your Child's Faith

Have you ever gotten a Christmas gift you could *use* and not just look at or play with? Like maybe you got a science kit, and you built a cool robot with it. Or maybe you got an art set, and you made a hundred beautiful pictures with it. The gifts God gives His children are gifts to be used. What are you really good at that God might want to use?

Holy Spirit, You are a gift, but You also give gifts! Please show me one (or a lot!) of the ways You've gifted me so I can let You use them to build Your projects! Amen.

46

WE CAN EXCEL IN THE SPIRIT'S GIFTS

If you really want spiritual gifts, choose the ones
that will be most helpful to the church.
1 Corinthians 14:12 CEV

The whole point of spiritual gifts
is that they help God do His work.
And the most important work
He wants to do with those gifts?

Build the church.

Some gifts are flashy and get attention,
and other gifts are quiet and secret.
But the place He most wants us
to use every gift the Holy Spirit gives?

In God's church.

Grow Your Faith

When you read 1 Corinthians 14, you'll see that these Christians were nuts about having spiritual gifts. Paul was glad they wanted them, but he encouraged them to keep in mind the purpose for those gifts: to build up the local church and serve its people. What gifts or talents, whether they're on the spiritual gifts lists or not, do you see as being extremely useful in building the local church?

Grow Your Child's Faith

What is something you are really good at? How can you use that gift to serve others and help your church? Ask if you can do it!

Holy Spirit, when You came to live in me, You brought some awesome tools for me to use. Please show me how I can use Your gifts to make my own church stronger and help the people in it to love God more. Amen.

47

THE HOLY SPIRIT PUTS HIS SEAL OF OWNERSHIP ON US

He put his mark on us to show that we are his, and he put his Spirit in our hearts to be a guarantee for all he has promised.
2 Corinthians 1:22 NCV

Have you ever written your name
on your coat or backpack
to show that it belongs to you?

God puts His mark on us too!

A king would melt wax and use a stamp
to seal important letters or papers
and show that they were really from him.

The Holy Spirit is God's seal on us!

Grow Your Faith

If the fullness of God's Spirit inside us is just a down payment for what is to come, then what will the full and total payment be like?

Grow Your Child's Faith

When a person becomes a Christian, the Holy Spirit comes into that person's heart. We are filled with Him. But even with how amazing that is, it's still just a first tiny taste of how fully we're going to be *in* God when we are in heaven. What do you think that might be like?

Holy Spirit, the fact that You are in my heart means God has marked me for His own. You want to be sure everyone knows I'm Yours. That's a great feeling. Amen.

48

THE HOLY SPIRIT GUIDES OUR SPIRITUAL LIFE

*The Spirit gives us desires that are the opposite
of what the sinful nature desires.*
Galatians 5:17 NLT

Your body and brain
are really good at living on earth.
But they can be pretty bad at obeying God.

When you become a Christian,
the Holy Spirit comes into you.
And the Spirit *really* wants to obey God.

What our earth bodies want
fights with what the Spirit wants;
so sometimes we do obey God and sometimes we don't.

Grow Your Faith

Does it seem strange that the Christian life consists of inner conflict and struggle? It might seem more logical for the Christian to be set free from sin and never stumble again. But that's not what we see, not with Simon Peter or Paul or Mother Teresa or Billy Graham. What we see are fallible people who tried to follow God and didn't always succeed. That's encouragement for the rest of us when we struggle!

Grow Your Child's Faith

What's something you know God wants you to do but you sometimes just can't make yourself do? What's something *wrong* you want to do even though you know God doesn't want you to? Can you feel that battle going on inside you? That's normal, and it means you're a Christian trying to love God. Keep up the fight!

Holy Spirit, sometimes I wish You would just take away everything in me that doesn't want to obey You. Please help me obey You more and more every day. Amen.

49

THE HOLY SPIRIT GIVES US FRUIT

The Holy Spirit produces this kind of fruit in our lives: love, joy, peace, patience, kindness, goodness, faithfulness, gentleness, and self-control.
Galatians 5:22–23 NLT

If you put a seed in good dirt
and give it the right amount
of water and sun,
a plant will grow.

If you put the Holy Spirit
inside a person
and give it time and love,
fruit of the Spirit will grow.

Grow Your Faith

What's one fruit of the Spirit that seems to grow well in your life? What's one you'd love to see a bigger harvest of? Ask the Holy Spirit to cultivate that fruit in you.

Grow Your Child's Faith

The Bible tells us that Jesus is like a vine and Christians are like branches. When the branches are joined to the vine, the life of the vine flows through them and fruit starts to grow on the branches. The more we let the Spirit flow through us, the more good fruit— like love and peace and joy—will grow in our lives.

Holy Spirit, I want to be a "tree" that grows all Your fruit all at once! Amen.

50

THE HOLY SPIRIT UNIFIES US

Make every effort to keep the unity of the
Spirit through the bond of peace.
Ephesians 4:3

All Christians around the world
and across the centuries
are joined into one giant family.

You have brothers in China
and sisters in Uganda.
You have God's family everywhere.

Of all people on earth,
Christians are called to be united—
one in the Spirit.

Grow Your Faith

Is there a Christian brother or sister with whom you are in a state of anger or broken relationship? Jesus gave His life to reconcile the world to God. We are to be reconcilers and peacemakers too. What's a step you could take toward peace?

Grow Your Child's Faith

Do you ever fight with your brother or sister or friend? Sometimes, the people we love the most can be the people we have the biggest arguments with. But under it all, we still love each other. It can be that way in God's family too. Is there anyone you're in a fight with or who is mad at you right now? How can the Holy Spirit help you make peace with that person?

Holy Spirit, I love that there are other kids all around the world who love You just as much as I do. I love that they speak to You in a bunch of different languages, and they feel You inside them in exactly the way I do! Help me be someone who makes peace wherever I go. Amen.

51

WE CAN SHARE
THE HOLY SPIRIT
WITH SINGING

When you meet together, sing psalms, hymns, and spiritual
songs, as you praise the Lord with all your heart.
Ephesians 5:19 CEV

In some wonderful way,
singing is both a gift *from* God
and a gift *to* God. So, sing.

Sing to the Lord.
Sing praises to the Lord.
Sing joyful praises to the Lord.
Sing joyful praises to the Lord with all your heart.

Grow Your Faith

We sing psalms collected from Israel's worship traditions, hymns
that teach doctrine with music, and spiritual songs as expressions
of the joy we have with God. The joy we have in the Spirit is not a
shallow emotion based on circumstances. Christians can be joyful
even in the midst of pain and suffering because of the confidence
we have in God.

Grow Your Child's Faith

What's your favorite church song? What do you like best about it? God absolutely loves it when you sing that song to Him. And He might just be singing along. How cool is that?

Holy Spirit, sometimes there is music in my heart just for You. Let my songs to You always be beautiful in Your ears. Amen.

52

THE BIBLE IS THE SWORD OF THE SPIRIT

*Take the helmet of salvation and the sword of
the Spirit, which is the word of God.*
Ephesians 6:17

Most of us don't live in war zones.
Most of us don't see fighting every day.
But every Christian is in a war,
and it's almost totally invisible.

What if God gave you a sword
so you could fight evil with the power of the Holy Spirit?
What if He gave you a whole set of armor
and called you to be one of His champions?

Guess what?
He did!

Grow Your Faith

As adult Christians, we can get so mired in the daily struggle of life, and even so discouraged by our own sin, that we leave our armor in the closet and our sword on the rack. Only Jesus is sinless, so He doesn't expect that of His soldiers. What He asks is that we suit up and call on the Holy Spirit to direct and empower us to keep fighting.

Grow Your Child's Faith

Could David have defeated Goliath without knowing God's words? No! He trusted in God, and God helped him kill the giant. David picked up the giant's huge sword and used it. Can you picture yourself as an awesome warrior hero with a sword of God? When you study God's Word, the Bible, the Spirit teaches you what you need to know to defeat your Enemy, Satan.

Holy Spirit, I love the idea that I could be a great hero for You. Please teach me how to use the Bible as a sword to fight and protect. Amen.